Pacific Coast Horns

Volume 2

76 TROMBONES
AND OTHER FAVORITES

TROMBONE

MUSIC MINUS ONE

3976

SUGGESTIONS FOR USING THIS MMO EDITION

We have tried to create a product that will provide you an easy way to learn and perform these compositions with a full ensemble in the comfort of your own home. The following MMO features and techniques will help you maximize the effectiveness of the MMO practice and performance system:

Because it involves a fixed accompaniment performance, there is an inherent lack of flexibility in tempo. We have observed generally accepted tempi, and always in the originally intended key, but some may wish to perform at a different tempo, or to slow down or speed up the accompaniment for practice purposes; or to alter the piece to a more comfortable key. For maximum flexibility, you can purchase from MMO specialized CD players & recorders which allow variable speed while maintaining proper pitch, and vice versa. This is an indispensable tool for the serious musician and you may wish to look into purchasing this useful piece of equipment for full enjoyment of all your MMO editions.

We want to provide you with the most useful practice and performance accompaniments possible. If you have any suggestions for improving the MMO system, please feel free to contact us. You can reach us by e-mail at *info@musicminusone.com*.

3976

CONTENTS

DISC A COMPLETE VERSION TRACK	DISC A MINUS VERSION TRACK	DISC B -12% SLOW MINUS TRACK	DISC B -25% SLOW MINUS TRACK		PAGE
	16	1		*Tuning*	
1	17	2	17	*Overture to Clementine*	4
2	18	3	18	*Fascinating Rhythm*	6
				Music Man Medley:	
3	19	4	19	*The Wells Fargo Wagon*	8
4	20	5	20	*Goodnight, My Someone*	8
5	21	6	21	*Gary, Indiana*	9
6	22	7	22	*Till There Was You*	9
7	23	8	23	*Pick-A-Little, Talk-A-Little/Good Night, Ladies*	9
8	24	9	24	*Lida Rose*	10
9	25	10	25	*Seventy Six Trombones*	11
10	26	11	26	*Funeral March for a Marionette*	14
11	27	12	27	*A String of Pearls*	16
12	28	13	28	*Bocoxe*	18
13	29	14	29	*Minnie the Moocher*	20
14	30	15	30	*Bist du bei mir*	21
15	31	16	31	*Sabre Dance*	22

ISBN 978-1-59615-786-6
1-59615-786-0

Trombone

Overture to Clementine

Ken Whitcomb

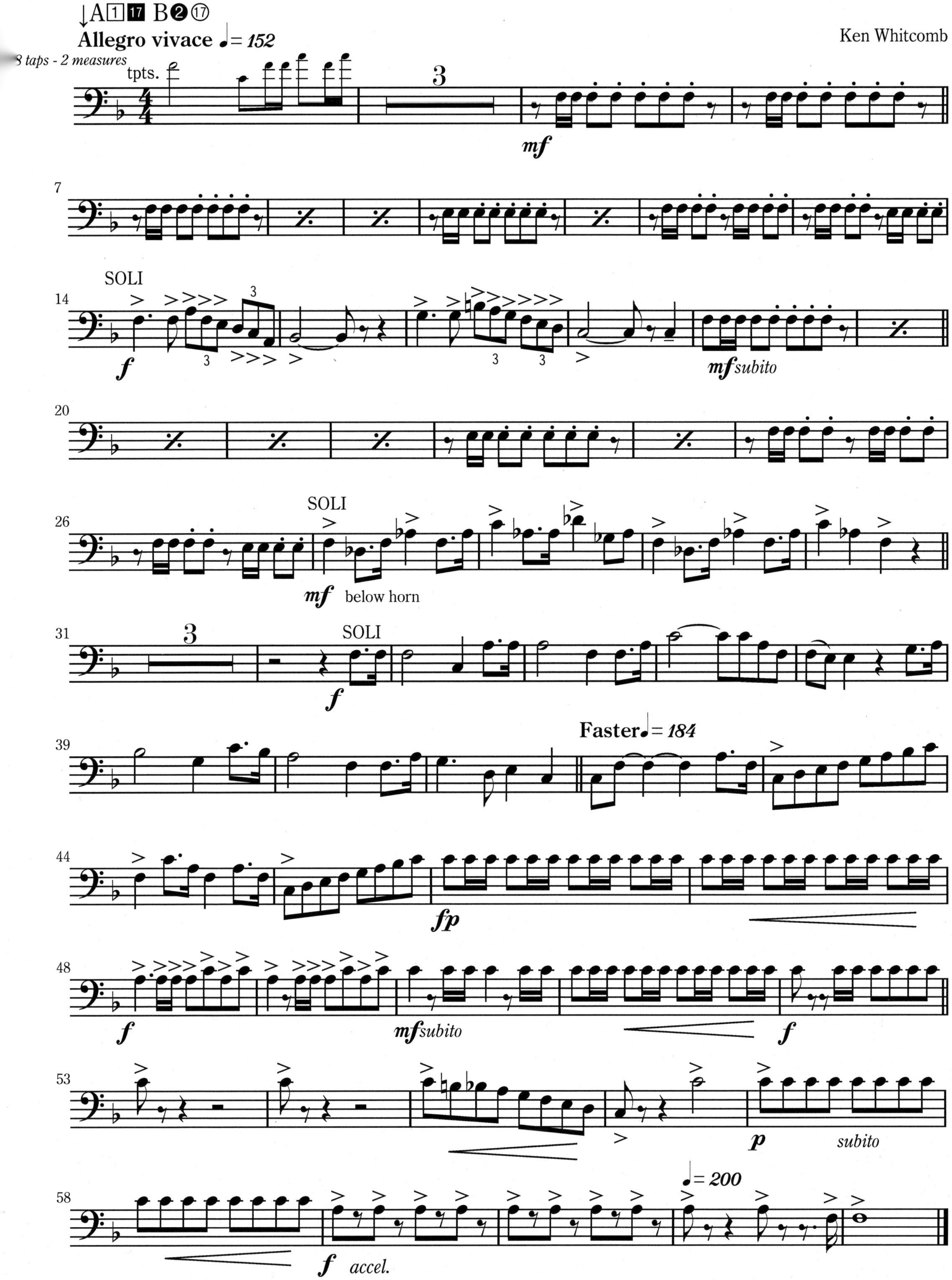

Fascinating Rhythm

Words by Ira Gershwin
Music by George Gershwin
arr. Chas Warren

Trombone

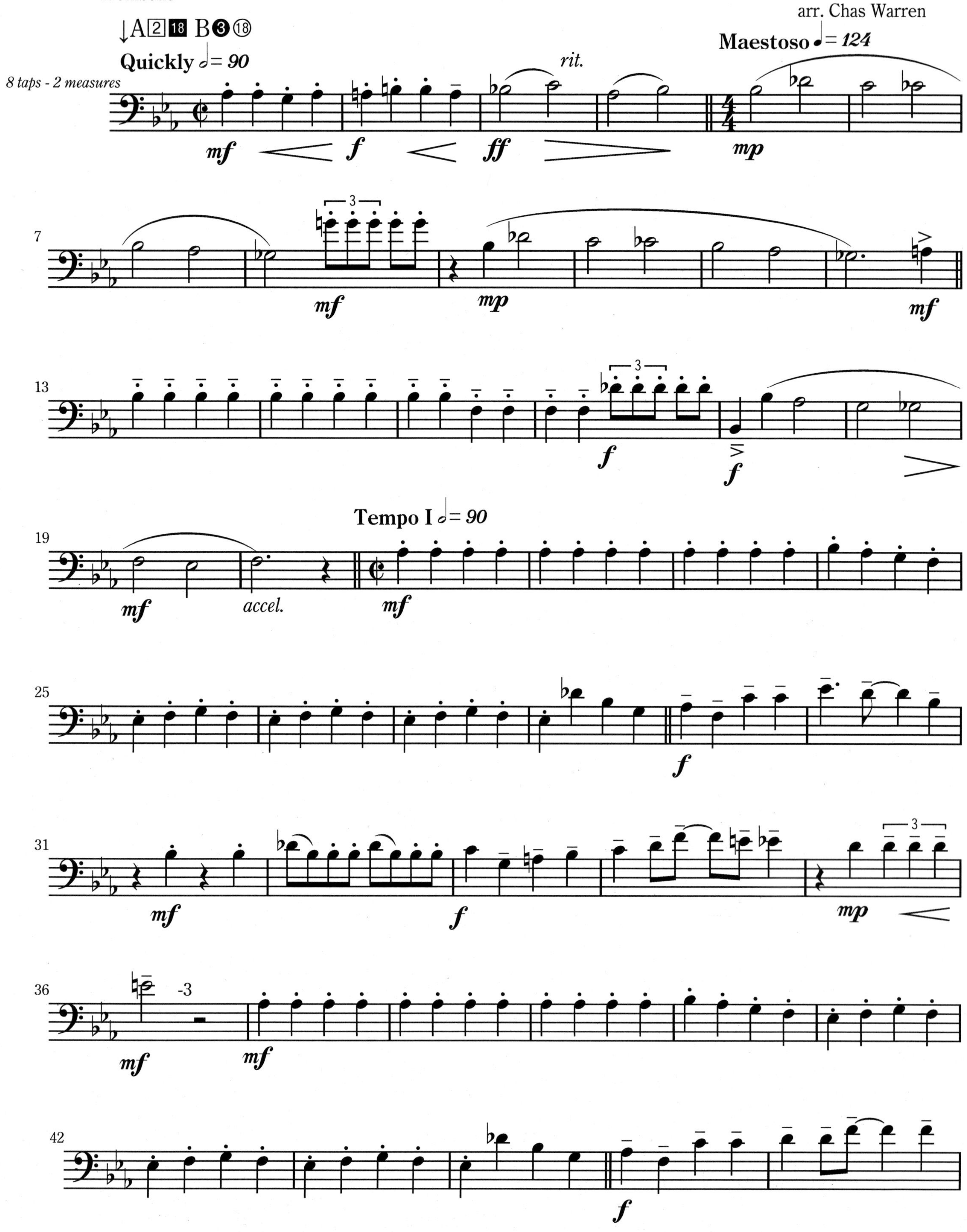

47
mf
53
mf
57
61
f
fp
fp
f
f
66
fp
pp
73
f
79
mf
SOLO
f
mf
84
-2
f

Trombone

Music Man Medley

Meredith Willson
arr. Chas Warren

↓A5 21 B6 21
"Gary, Indiana" 12/8 feel
Soft Shoe Bounce ♩= 108
69
mp
mf
mp
74
SOLO
mf
p
mf
p
81
mp
SOLI
mf
SOLI
mp
86
mf
mp
92
3
rit.
↓A6 22 B7 22
Moderately Fast ♩= 100 ""Till There Was You"
SOLO
mf legato e express.
101
(mf)
107
113
SOLI
mf
3
121
SOLO
mf
rit.
A Tempo
mf
Slower
♩= 84
127
poco rit.
↓A7 23 B8 23
Lively ♩= 128 "Pick-A-Little, Talk-A-Little"
tpts.
7
V. S.

138
mf
143
under tuba
p
148
SOLO
3
f
153
under horn
ord.
p
158
under tuba
Tpt.
"Goodnight, Ladies"
SOLI
mf
163
170
mp
4
A 8 24 B 9 24
"Lida Rose"
molto rubato
Li-da Rose I'm
179
home a- gain Rose With-out etc.
184
In Tempo
191
In Tempo
rit.

198
203
In Tempo
rit.
210
217
224
229
234
A la marcia ♩. = 120
242
tuba
"Seventy Six Trombones"
SOLO
mf
250
f
259

V. S.

obbligato
267
mf
277
SOLO
mf
285
f subito mf
293
f subito
mf
301
f subito mp
309
poco a poco cresc.
f
ff
f subito
317
326
obbligato
ff
334
342
ff

Funeral March of a Marionette

Trombone

Charles Gounod
adulterated by Chas Warren

58
63
70
LEAD
mf
76
Cannon
4
snap fingers
84
mf
mf
89
94
LEAD
f
mp cresc.
99
ord.
mf
f
LEAD
mp cresc.
ord.
104
mf
f
SOLO
ord.
mp
110
LEAD
mp cresc.
mf
f
mp

A String of Pearls

Trombone

↓A 11 27 B 12 27

Tempo di Mollusk ♩ = *160*

by Jerry Gray
arr. Chas Warren

40
p subito
mp
46
f
mf
mp
52
mf
mp
58
64
70
f
f
p
D. S. al Coda
74
mf
f
79
fp

Bocoxe

Trombone

Baden Powell
arr. Buttery/Warren

67
SOLO
mp
75
SOLO
cresc. poco a poco
f
mf
83
3
mf dim.
94
mp
104
114
124
f
mf
133
fp
cresc.
f
dim. molto
niente
6
147
mp
p

Minnie the Moocher

Trombone

Words & Music by
Cab Calloway & Irving Mills
arr. Chas Warren

Bist du bei mir

(IF THOU BE NEAR)

Trombone

J. S. Bach
trans. Chas Warren

Sabre Dance

Trombone

Aram Khachaturian
arr. Paul Chauvin

(LEAD)
SAVAGE!!

MUSIC MINUS ONE
50 Executive Boulevard
Elmsford, New York 10523-1325
1.800.669.7464 (U.S.)/914.592.1188 (International)

www.musicminusone.com
e-mail: info@musicminusone.com

MMO 3976

Pub. No. 0945

Printed in Canada